Unwritten Poems
and other Muses

Skylar Martin

BookLeaf
Publishing
India | USA | UK

Presentation by *BookLeaf Publishing*

Web: www.bookleafpub.com

E-mail: info@bookleafpub.com

ISBN: 9789357444378

First edition 2022

DEDICATION

This is dedicated to my inner circle of friends, the memories we have shared are the main inspirations for these poems.

ACKNOWLEDGEMENT

These poems would not have been possible without the support of my family and close friends. Specifically, the support of my loving husband Thomas, my mother Brittany, Father Shawn, and my sister Bronwyn.

One Warm Night

Smiled so hard I split my lip
Emotive a slow drip drip
Cracked teeth
We press our sides together
Defining sisterhood in the unknown
Blood juice leaks from our lips
Us bitches really love fermented grapes
Two sides gemini
I'd rather pee with you
Than face the crowd alone
Smiled so hard I chipped a tooth
Gravity came a little too soon
Stiffened legs imbroglios
At the boastful moon

Circe's Vows

Deep in my living quarters
Upon my hearth
Lies a loom
Spun from far away sheep
It's wool
Dyed prairie grass
It weaves a symmetrical constellation
Each knot strings my chest to yours
And yours to mine
This loom offers eternity on borrowed time
A story woven by the stars
Our life mapped out together

November 2020

I am growing quite weary
From pushing out these opal tears

Coming of Age

Tonight,
I am on the brink of infinity
Celestial stars wrap my cerebrum in lavender
soaked dreams
Fibers in my muscles threaten to split open
My cells combust
I embark on this universal expansion
My stomach carries the birth of the sun
I am adorned in drapes of solar winds
Shifting from this stage to the next
Feminine shape shifter
Lunar transitions
To womanhood

Nocturnal River

Together we link arms
And dipped our toes into liquid obsidian
As cold, slick
As the sweat on my brow
We perch on a wooden carcass
Smoke billows out our lungs
And I finally understand the desire for infinity

Melancholy Honey

What do you do
When depression has found you on your
honeymoon
It travelled six hours to find me
Through mountain valleys carved by dynamite
Underneath wet pressed greens where spiders
lay their claim
To my cabin tucked aside
To me
Pressed in white linens
The colour white has a new meaning to me
If I am not careful
I will be preserved in melancholy
Crystalized like old honey
In moments like this
What can I do?
But force coffee down my throat
And stick to the creek

Death by Perseus

With one flick
You hook into another part of me
Diving deep in soft flesh
A cross stitch
Embeds trauma
These needles create a constant blister
This flaked skin a permanent
I lye naked in the temple
Waiting for the next great betrayal

Blood in Anti-Gravity

I always wondered how your blood would look
in anti-gravity
Does it betray the body?
Will you still bloat, purple and blue?
When the time comes
I hope your face is marred
That it twists, flesh compressed on flesh
Have you seen the thing?
Blood thirsty tycoons
You abandon your first mother
Leave the rest of us to contend with a planet on
fire
To satisfy the megalomania
I imagine your blood thinned out
Dried and cured
Rancid meat
Prepped for strenuous decomposition
Your body will receive no reprieve in the next
There will be no ceremony
No family or resting place
Your vessel is simply expelled

As you succumb to space
The cosmos pull this expanded ego into uncaring
stars
Incredulous
As you are lost to eternity

Another Lockdown

I guess there's no point in dwelling
These thoughts will bury me like a silk spread
An entanglement of toilet paper and mold
Stuffing my lungs into oblivion
I can't survive another lockdown
I can't continue to mourn what I have lost
Time to embrace catatonia

October

Oh how I mourn you October
Your rolling tongues of burnt orange paint the
prairie
You adorn death in yellow
A golden field replicating the after life
Oh how I love the frost bit air
Causes my lungs to pause
The season of Demeter
The harvest signifies the divine feminine
Soon Persephone will return to her prison
And I will lye bundled
Waiting for Jack Frost

Fly

Last night
I was visited by deaths friend
Like me, he was looking for shelter from the
rain
He wore a coat of fog
Spores emanate from yellow wings
The sweet smell of rot his cologne
The promise of eternity a comfort
He offers me a cigarette of mugwort sealed with
purple wax
I wrap myself in a blanket of leaves
A pillow of hoarfrost brings a numbing
transition
Lead me to the frozen light

Back Alley Tattoos

I first learned about the trade industry through
back door tattoos
A secret garden in rich suburbia
I flick my poems up my sleeve
Ready to offer my services for a rose hip
The artist, the gatekeeper
Bathed in hallucinogenic luminescence
Drunk stooped in a corner
The light of the room a thick heat wave
I struggle to focus
I want to be apart of this fairy circle
Spore sanctity

Prairie Highways

Death came riding up the highway
Leaves bloody prints on the shoulder
A headless horseman
Dusts the road with Ravens beaks
Spreading the stories of the lost ones
He wears an emblem of dead twigs
Encouraging the arrival of the winter solstice
To bring the world to its knees

What Happened in Grade 10

You sneak within the crevices of my cerebrum
Spy behind my eyes
Caress my frontal lobes with your tongue
Vile creature
Lurk and heave within the worst parts of me
You offered me something once
Promises of candy and silk
I feel the cold sting of your betrayal every time I
yearn for touch
You have left my body in flames
Plucked my fruit as if it was yours to take
Reflected entitlement of your father
And his father
I pray you do not have a son
Beg the moon with her stars to end this cycle
Not just for me
For the hunted

Healing

He filled my core with lead
Over time it dispenses into my body
A painful drip
This, is healing

The Beldam

In a grey room,
Filled with chalk and dust
A spider spins her web
Her fingers numb, brittle with time
She weaves a new world
Filled with cotton candy clouds
A sun that never fades
Tasty tricks
Husks of flies from her last meal lye with their
legs in the air
She has forgotten them
So she focuses on the web
Spun for the next lonely fly

Samhain

Tonight,
We can be anything
The veil is lifted
The pumpkins we harvested to butcher
Sit on our porch like a death mask
Ward off evil
To lead our lost ones to the front porch
Cinnamon incense burns a hole in my favourite
sweater
I can see Orion
But no Sirius
Frost dresses dead leaves
Quilts for sleeping insects
Tonight,
The veil is lifted
And we can be anything

Paper Boy Pants

Erratic folds
Tucked in at the front of my drawer
I own two pairs
In burgundy and black
I bring out the burgundy when I feel adventurous
The grace of an elastic waist
I can eat my pasta with no disgrace

Covid Youth

The North wind pinches rose cheeks
We gather in a snow coat huddle
My feet went numb some time ago
I suppose this is it
Our youth is charcoal in a pit
My early twenties tired embers
Fatigue stains an over used thermos
As we observe the choreography of flames

House Party

Tiny orbs
Gather around a glowing flame
Warmth and comfort linger
Like an old vice
Sweet incense baths my lungs
In copal and sage
Mother Russia in my cup
There was a time when we shared drinks
Pasted wallflower
The smooth surface a comfort
I take a sip
And try to blend in

Over the Garden Wall

It began with a frog hunt
A witches gathering
And a tape
Pumpkin purgatory
A voice in the night
Replicates rustling leaves
The wind carries it's melodies
Patient is the night
A tiny star leads them back home
A small price for the ferry man